Taking it from the top

Why a hole in the ground?

The Eden Project site, 1998

The Eden Project was built in a giant hole which had reached the end of its previous life - as a china clay pit. When Alan and Enid arrived there were no buildings, no plants and no soil, just a soggy crater. The Eden team built giant greenhouses and a global garden here to show that people can change things for the better.

The Eden Project site, 2002

… us to … The wild places, such as the world's forests, help control the world's climate. Some plants, grown as crops, give us our foods, fuels, medicines and materials. At Eden we explore how to care for the wild plants and the crops. We need to look after these things because they look after us.

Why a project?

Because we're always trying out new things to help look after the planet and the people on it and sharing what we find out. Tell us your ideas too! Eden is always changing. Check out the picture taken in 2002. What's changed since then?

Introductions

Meet Sniff

Meet Digger

Tick the box when you have found these places.

The Metal Giant in the Outdoor Biome

The Nest outside the Core

The Log behind the Core

The Giant Xylophone, Wild Cornwall, Outdoor Biome

Contact Sniff at:
Sniff, Eden Project, Bodelva, St Austell, Cornwall, PL24 2SG,
email: sniff@edenproject.com

The Outdoor Biome

Welcome to the great outdoors

When you see the dashes, fill in the blanks!

Go down the zigzag path, past age-old ferns to the WEEEman and the crops that feed the whole world. Look out for plants grown for food, fuel, medicines and materials...

Explore the great outdoors

Across the site and in the next few pages help Alan and Enid find the plants that make tea, rope, cooking oil, paper, medicines, bread, popcorn…even coal.

Flowerless Garden

Plants which grew in dinosaur times rotted down to make C _ _ _ Today we burn fossil fuels (coal, oil etc.) which release a gas called carbon dioxide (CO_2) into the air. It forms a gassy blanket around the earth and causes climate change.

Ferns grew in the days of the dinosaurs.

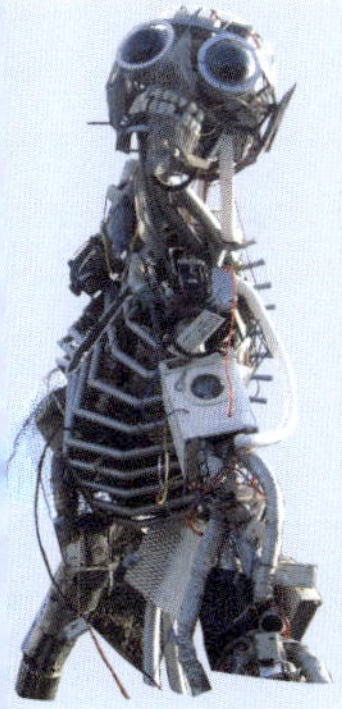

WEEEman

This **W**aste, **E**lectrical and **E**lectronic **E**quipment man is made of the stuff one person throws away in their lifetime. Crikey. Hope Enid recycled that old TV.

What are his teeth made of?

\- - - -

Plant Spotter

Tick the box if you find the plant

Fern

Banana

Who am I?

Who am I?

....

....

Crops that Feed the World

Wheat, rice, maize, potatoes, bananas and beans.

Digger match-up

Can you help Digger match the plant to the product?

Time to Relax ...

Past the flowers and sweet pea fence to the garden full of magical outdoor rooms, stop off in the willow play area and then onto the Bakery by the Sense of Taste garden...

Draw your favourite thing in the garden

The Garden of Senses

See how many different colour flowers and leaves you can find in the garden. One for every colour of the rainbow? Red, orange,

_ _ _ _ _ _

green, blue, indigo, violet.

Come on in and play away

... And play a game

A Sense of Taste

Depending on the time of year, see if you can find any of these plants growing. Our chefs use these plants but there isn't enough to feed everyone so we buy the rest in from local growers. Local so the food doesn't have to travel far, less lorries, less pollution, less CO_2, helping to fight climate change.

Digger match-up

What a cropper

Go from the Orchard, past the Bee – bzzz – past the Cornish Crops and round the corner to the Beer exhibit, the Tea Ship and up to the Global Gardens. Phew!

Alan and Enid are delighted! They've found honey, local vegetables, exotic vegetables, apples, beers and a nice cup of tea. Can you find them too?

The Orchard

What fruit come from these trees?

_ _ _ _ _

Pollination

Bees pollinate flowers and get a reward of nectar in return. Bees make . . . ?

_ _ _ _ _

Cornish Crops

Name a vegetable grown in Cornwall?

....

Beer and Brewing

What plants are used to make beer?

_ _ _ _ _ _

and _ _ _ _

(Clue: Look closely at the big wooden poles)

Tea

Tea was once brought to the UK from China on fast sailing ships called Clippers.

Global Gardens

See if you can find any vegetables growing here that you have never seen before. We found out about them from gardeners all over the world.

In our Gardens For Life project (which you can find out about in the blue shed), schools in the UK, Africa and India exchange gardening tips. We told a school in Kenya that we had whitefly in our garden. They replied, "we had an elephant in ours!"

Kenya

Plant Spotter

Match the picture to the plant and its product.

1. Lavender for Alan's scented soap
2. Cauliflower for Enid's tasty stir fry
3. Raspberries to have with cream
4. Barley for Alan's beer

The West Side

Up and round you go, peep through the hemp fence, past the Metal Giant to the Industrial Flame Plant, over to Myth and Folklore then up again to Wild Cornwall and over to the giant tyre.

Crops for a Material World

Check out the little greenhouses. See if you can find three more things that plants are made into:

1. Clothes

2. Plant plastic knives and forks

3 ....

4 ....

5 ....

Hemp

Alan's delighted. He's found hemp that can be made into clothes, oils, ropes, fuels, paper and plastic. Here we've made it into a fence.

Fuels

Enid uses wood as fuel instead of coal. Why? Because burning fossil fuels (coal, oil, gas) puts carbon dioxide gas (CO_2) around the earth like a gassy blanket and adds to climate change.

Life, stories and rocks

Myth and Folklore

Try out the labyrinth inside the willow dome. It's an ancient pattern that takes you on a journey. Start at the opening and wind your way into the middle. Before you turn to retrace your steps, stop, have a think, then begin your journey out the way you went in. Do you feel anything different? Mazes are different – they get you lost!

Wild Cornwall

Peep into the walls, you'll find carvings of plants that are so rare you may never see them in the wild. Look closely at the living plants. How many different shapes of leaves can you spot in one minute?

....

Mining the Earth

Take a trip underground behind the giant tyre. See if you can find three more things that rocks give us.

1. Gold rings

2. Talcum powder

3 ....

4 ....

5 ....

Gardens round the Core

Medicines made from plants

Take a walk round the Core from left to right. Find plants for dyes, follow secret routes through the Plants for Paper garden, visit the Spiral Garden and our baby forest.

Health

Enid's found her medicine cupboard: rows and rows of plants that are used to make medicines.
Name a plant that is used to make medicine:

....

....

Dyes

Alan's found a whole load of plants to dye his clothes. Which plant makes which colour?

Red ....

Blue ....

Yellow ....

Paper

Paper is made from all the plants you can see growing here.

The Spiral Garden

Loads of ideas in here for your own gardens and a growing spiral made from willow.

- Grow a rainbow out of different coloured flowers
- Make a mosaic out of broken china
- *Sarracenia,* grow a plant that catches flies.

- *Arisarum proboscideum,* grow a plant that looks like a mouse's tail.

Timber

Boats, oars, chairs, doors,
Homes, piles, sticks to walk miles,
Frames for Morgans, pipes for organs,
Artificial legs and tent pegs.
See which wood is best for what
What have you got that's made of wood?

....

....

....

....

Red spruce wood made the roof of the Core

Eden through the year

Spring

Freaky Nature

Summer

Den building

Autumn

Halloweden

Winter

Ice skating

Change one letter at a time to go from WARM to COLD

WARM in the Rainforest Biome

_ _ _ _ This wriggly creature lives in the soil

_ _ _ _ Many letters make one and there are many in one letter

_ _ _ _ Also called rope, and handy for den building

COLD on the ice rink

The Core

Inside the Core

The Core was designed to be the shape of a sunflower and the size of a spaceship. Don't forget to visit the inner chamber to find the Seed.

The Plant Engine

The glass domes attached to the big glass bubble contain clues that show how plants look after our world and keep us alive.

Can you help Alan and Enid match the jars below to the list below?

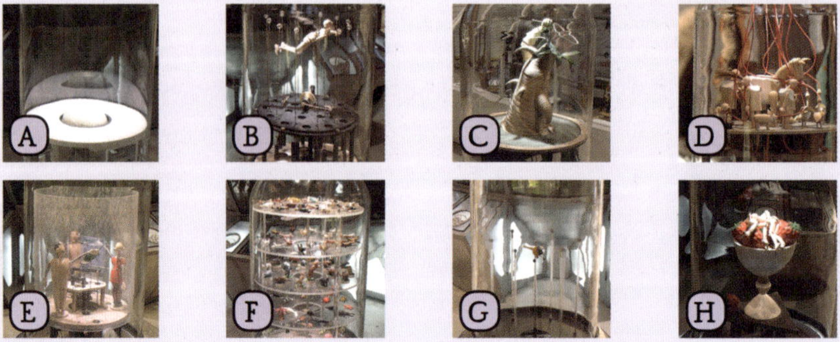

- ◯ They make us fresh air to breathe
- ◯ They keep our climate under control.
- ◯ They recycle our waste
- ◯ They support animals and bugs (biodiversity)
- ◯ They clean our water
- ◯ They give us ideas to copy (biomimicry)
- ◯ They suck CO_2 out of the air
- ◯ They give us inspiration

Tick them when you've done them!

- ◯ Use the biggest nutcracker in the world
- ◯ Guess the next number: 0 1 1 2 3 5 8 13 21 ....
- ◯ Count how many spirals there are in each direction.

The Seed

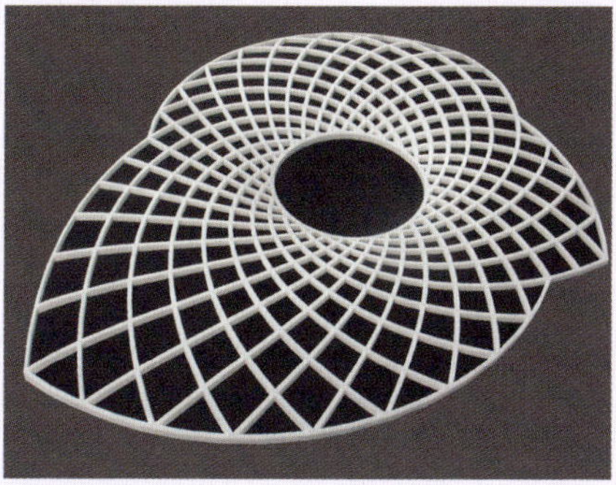

(The spirals that go to the left and to the right in sunflowers, pineapples and our roof, are two consecutive numbers in this sequence)

Digger finds the Eden Deli!

The café upstairs has loads of jars showing you which foods give you which vitamins and minerals.
You can draw your favourite food on the blackboard.
Mine's a bone.

Activity page

Crossword

Across

1. The dog with an appetite
5. The plant with seeds like a giant bottom
6. The fruit that sports people like

Down

2. The tree that makes our wellies
3. The plant that makes chocolate
4. The giant robot made of rubbish

Digger on food

Lemonade

Coffee

Bread

Coffee plant

Wheat

Lemon

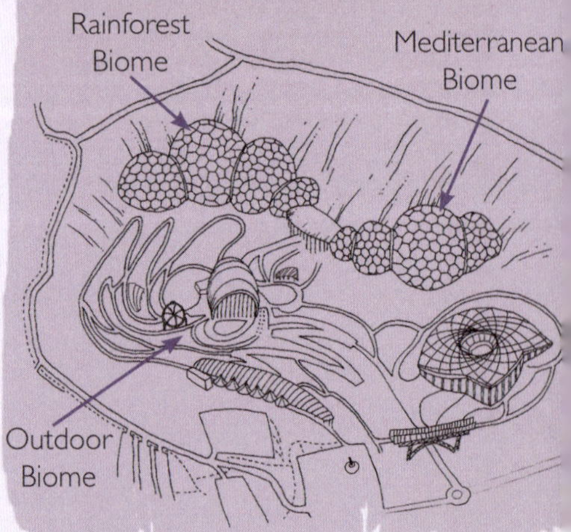

The Rainforest Biome

Welcome to the largest rainforest in captivity

Rainforests are in the humid tropics regions of the world, found near the equator.

The Lookout

Look up … on days when it's not too hot you can climb up into the Rainforest Lookout where you can:

Look down … on the whole Biome. A piece of primary forest the size of this Biome is destroyed in the wild every 10 seconds.

The red star on the map shows the entrance to the Lookout

Look out … for Sniff who is looking for ideas of how to help save the rainforest.

Tropic Trader

Digger helps Alan & Enid find out about tropical food

Give Digger a hand, trek through these hot, steamy places to help Alan and Enid find many of the plants they are looking for.

Which of the following plants come from the humid tropics? Put a circle round them and check your answer with the Eden team.

Cocoa for chocolate bars

Coffee beans for coffee drinks

Bamboo for spoons and bowls

Mango for smoothies

Bananas for smoothies

Wheat for bread

Potatoes for baking

Grapes for wine

Lemon for lemonade

Islands and the East

Cross the bridges and follow the winding paths through the tropical islands ... walk round the hairpin bend and up into Malaysia

Coco de Mer seed, awesome!

Alan and Enid visit the tropical islands – home to rare, wild plants including the Coco de Mer which has seeds like a giant bottom! Building lots of new houses and roads, planting more crops and having loads of tourists on small islands can destroy the local island plants. Eden worked with scientists and local people in the Seychelles islands to help save rare plants, like this *Balsamine sauvage*, from extinction.

Mangroves are important for islands and islanders. They grow in the mud between the land and __ __ __, help protect the coast from storms and act as a natural barrier against tsunamis.

The Malaysian Garden

Enid likes the house. It's made out of plants and it's on stilts to keep out of floods and snakes (don't worry there's none in here). Alan recognises the chillies but needs Digger's help with other plants in the garden.

Digger finds a magic tree!

The miracle tree (*Moringa*) is often found in gardens in the tropics. It has edible leaves, fruit, flowers and shoots, its seeds are used as water filters and its oils for oiling delicate clockwork devices. Digger also finds some rice growing opposite the garden in a muddy pool.

Moringa, the miracle tree

Plant Spotter

Tick the box when you find each plant

Chillies

Moringa

Rice

Mangroves

From West Africa to...

Round the elbow bend to the post that says West Africa then take the upper or lower road through South America.

The totems

Why does this sculpture look burnt? The timber it is made from was recycled from a part of Falmouth docks which was destroyed by _ _ _ _. This timber originally came from trees from West Africa!

Totems by West African sculptor El Anatsui

Trees that feed the soil

Some of the trees here are 'legumes'. They make food out of air for the plant.

Tropical South America

Visit the cassava house on the bottom path

In South America local people who live in the rainforest often eat cassava. The thick roots have to be grated and washed and a paste squeezed out using a tipiti (below). It takes ages to prepare dinner.

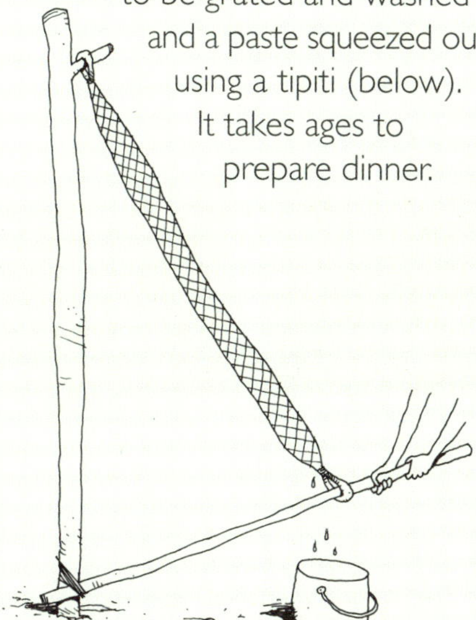

See the rainforest paintings and visit the Lookout on the top path*

Francisco Montes Shuna and his wife Yolanda Panduro Baneo, a medicine man and woman from Peru, painted some wonderful pictures (on the wall on the top path by the waterfall) to show the spirits that they see in rainforest plants.

*N.B. There are steps at the end of this path and 115 steps up to the Lookout too.

Crops of the Humid Tropics

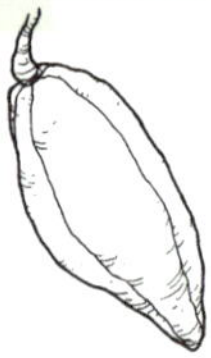
Cocoa

Sugar cane

Coffee

Oil palm

Oil palm

Sugar cane

Cocoa

Pineapple

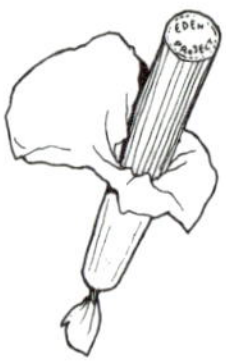
Stick of rock

Cake

Mango Smoothie

Cashew nuts

Under the arch to Crops and Cultivation where you will find a whole range of plants that we use every day that come from the tropics.

Mango

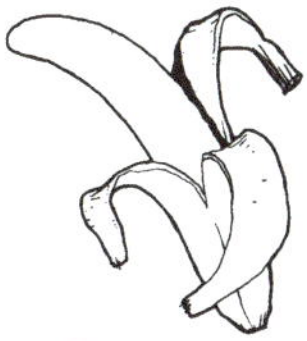
Banana

Pineapple

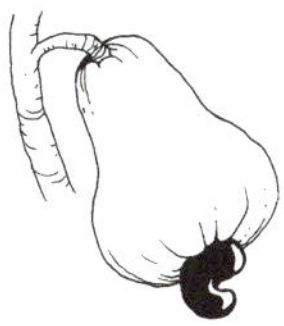
Cashew

Cashew

Mango

Coffee

Banana

Banana split

Chocolate

Pineapple pizza

Coffee

....

....

Rainforest quiz

Alan, Enid, Sniff and Digger search the Biome looking for clues to help them with the great Rainforest Quiz.

Q1. Cocoa makes chocolate. How does cocoa grow?

a. In little red beans along the branches of a bush

b. On trees in big yellow pods full of purple beans

c. Inside swollen roots under the ground

Q2. Name one way the rainforests help to keep us alive.

....

Q3. Which of the following can be made from bamboo: bowls, bridges, spoons, paper, clothes, buildings, scaffolding, stir fry

Q4. How can you help save the rainforest?

a. By telling your friends how it keeps us alive

b. By buying rainforest-friendly products

c. By supporting organisations that are working to save the rainforest

Q5. How do rainforests get their name?

....

Q6. When we put something made from the white liquid of a rainforest tree on our feet what are we doing?

....

Q7. What rainforest fruit feeds many people in the tropics and is often eaten by sportspeople to give them long-lasting energy?

....

Q8. What type of rainforest tree can vegetable cooking oil be made from?

....

Q9. Why don't orang-utans like biscuits containing palm oil (vegetable oil)?

....

The Spice of Life quiz

See if you can find the following spices in the Spice Boat:

- [x] Saffron
- [x] Pepper
- [x] Cloves
- [x] Vanilla
- [x] Ginger
- [ ] Paprika

Which sentence goes with which spice?

a. The name of this spice comes from the Latin, *clavus*, which means nail.

C L O V E S

b. This spice is used to make biscuits called

G I N G E R bread men.

c. This spice makes Cornish buns yellow. S A F F R O N

d. This spice is used to flavour ice cream. V A N I L L A

e. Columbus was looking for this spice when he discovered America. It now sits next to the salt on our table.

P E P P E R

f. A red powder used to make spicy sausages.

P A P R I K A

Check the drawers on the Spice Boat to get more clues

The Mediterranean Biome

Welcome to the Mediterranean regions

Walk to the golden path, through scented herbs and gnarled olives. Past the vines and dancing metal figures to the fig tree.

These regions, also called the Warm Temperate regions, have hot, dry summers and cool wet winters. We use sun cream and sun hats and drink cool drinks when we're on holiday in these sunny places. The plants avoid sunburn and thirst by having waxy or hairy leaves and scented oils. Look at the size of their leaves compared to the Rainforest Biome plants. Why do you reckon they are smaller?..

The Mediterranean

Enid loves her Mediterranean food; bit of olive oil, few herbs. The path behind her and beneath your feet has some images of doves, one for each Mediterranean country which grows olives.
How many can you count? ……

Food facts from a friendly dog

Two fruits, two facts. Which goes with which?

1. The flowers are found on the inside of these fruits and they are pollinated by tiny wasps. Bzzz!

2. These fruits have a crown at their tip. The juicy red seeds can be released by cutting the fruit in half, putting them face down and bashing with a spoon. Messy!

☐ Fig

☐ Pomegranate

Visit South Africa...

Follow your nose to the sights and scents of South Africa, go round the bend and head for the Harley motorbike.

The Fynbos fire flowers

There's loads of really unusual and rare plants in this part of South Africa. Some times these really dry areas go up in flames. New plants grow out of the burned earth.

Namaqualand

...and California

Cowboys

The plants in the "chaparral" are tough and spiky. Horse riders wear 'chaps' to protect their legs.

... and Indians

The Native Americans who reached California about 15,000 years ago found so many wild plants and animals to eat that they had no need to develop farming.

Alan finds his Agave

With spiky leaves with long fibres for brushes, sacking and twine, their flowers make soap and their sap a boozy drink: tequila.

Crops from the Mediterranean regions

Match the plant to the product below and tick them off if you find them in the Biome.

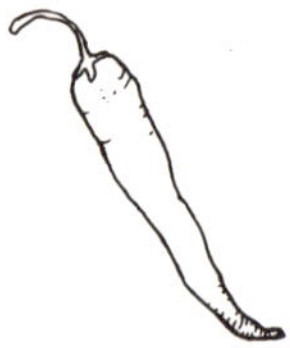
Chilli

Lemon

Thyme

Tomato

Lemon tree

Olive tree

Peach Tree

Grape vine

Olive oil

Lemonade

Curry

Tomato ketchup

Step into Crops and Cultivation where you will find a whole range of plants that we use every day that come from the Mediterranean regions of the world.

Olive

Grape

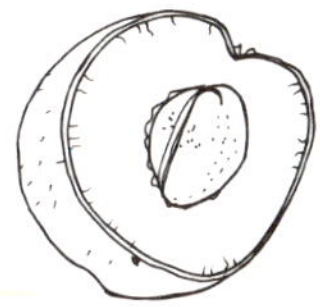
Peach

Thyme bush

Chilli

Tomato plant

Can of peaches

Wine

Thyme on pizza

....

....

Mediterranean quiz

Alan, Enid, Sniff and Digger search the Biome looking for clues to help them with the great Mediterranean Quiz.

Q1. What part of the cork tree gives us cork?

C O R K

Q2. Name two animals that live in cork oak forests.

C R A N E

P I G

Q3. Find two fruits in the Mediterranean orchard.

....

....

Q4. Which fruit, full of Vitamin C, may help to keep colds at bay?

....

Q5. What are we?

Jellied, dried or juiced
Or trampled with bare feet
To make wines from vines
Hick! Dry or sweet?

_ _ _ _ _ _ _

Q6. In the vines you will find a bull, what's his name?

_ _ _ _ _ _ _ _ _

Q7. The Mediterranean is warm and sunny, what do farmers have to add to make the plants grow?

....

Q8. Today we use olive oil as a healthy cooking oil. What was it used for in the days before electricity?

....

Eden facts

BIG PITCH
In the beginning this disused china clay pit was 60m deep. It is the area of 35 football pitches.

HUGE
Overall the Biomes contain 625 hexagons, the largest being 11 metres across.

DISASTER!
When Eden was built 43 million gallons of water rained into the pit in 90 days: our engineers had to come up with an amazing drainage system.

BUBBLES
Three layers of ETFE (ethylenetetrafluoroethylene) transparent foil form inflated pillows 2m deep in each of the hexagons. ETFE weighs less than 1% of the same area of glass.

SIZE
The world's largest conservatories – they weigh only slightly more than the air they contain.

SOIL
In a pit which had no soil the team made 83,000 tonnes of it – using china clay waste and organic waste.

SOLAR POWER
The Core is powered partly by the sun.

GROUND POWER
We're aiming to build a geothermal plant for power and heat; drilling over 4km down into the earth.

HOW MANY PLANTS?
Over a million plants, of about 6000 different types.

COPPER
The roof of the Core is covered with copper, 0.6mm thick, and was responsibly sourced from one mine in America.

SCORCHING
Unlike glass, the ETFE that covers the Biomes transmits ultraviolet rays, which means you can get a suntan indoors. Don't forget to cover up.

TALLEST
Tallest tree in Rainforest Biome: the kapok tree at over 19m.

SAVE WATER
We use rainwater/groundwater to water the plants and flush the loos.

PEOPLE
We have around a million visitors a year (and over 500 staff), and a further 2 million visit our website.

Eden's projects

Eden creates gardens, exhibitions, events and projects that explore how people can work together, care for the natural world and change things for the better. www.edenproject.com

Projects for people

All about getting people together, because it's a lot easier to change things when you work with others.

The Big Lunch: bringing people together with their neighbours for a few hours of community, friendship and fun.

Green Foundation: sharing ideas with businesses – ideas about working together, working with nature, and how to produce less CO_2.

Projects for places

All about sharing ideas to help leave places better than we found them – like this china clay pit, and like the rainforest.

Projects for climate

A whole range of projects looking at how we can help reduce CO_2 emissions and tackle climate change.

Clear about Carbon exhibit in the Core

Activities

The food in our cafés is sourced locally

This is to reduce "food miles" – i.e. the distance it has to travel, which saves fuel and reduces the CO_2 released into the air that contributes to climate change.

We love fruit too: we grow it, serve it and even name our car parks after it. Why? Because it's good for you and it's delicious. Here's a fruity example from each Biome for you to colour in.

Oranges, full of vitamin C, to keep off colds.

Bananas, full of slow-release energy, to keep you going.

An apple a day keeps the doctor away (the guy who invented this saying lived to be 92!).

Which Biome would you find each fruit in?

....

Did you spot..?

A wooden ship in the tea exhibit, Outdoor Biome.

A pole that hops grow up, Outdoor Biome.

A spice boat in the Rainforest Biome.

A cocoa pod in the Rainforest Biome.

A big bull in the Mediterranean Biome.

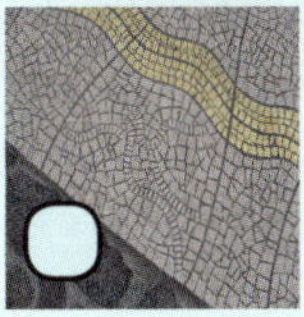

A mosaic dove in the Mediterranean Biome.

If you've done it, tick the box:

- ☐ Made something in a workshop
- ☐ Listened to a story
- ☐ Recycled some rubbish in the bins
- ☐ Walked the labyrinth in Myth and Folklore

If not, don't despair; here's how to make your own!

You can draw a seven-circuit labyrinth like this one. It is based on a "seed pattern". The seed pattern is a cross with four right angles within the ones created by the cross, and a dot in each right angle.

Start at the top of the cross, draw a curved line to join it to the first available line or dot. Keep going until you have the whole labyrinth.

... and if you've already left Eden and gone back home see if you can spot the images somewhere in this book. We look forward to seeing you again!

Eden's 11 top tips
for a better world

1 Do stuff: Don't waste it, turn it off, turn it down, do it less, recycle, repair, reuse.

2 Be hopeful: Just that. Believe you can help make the world a great place.

3 Learn about your life: A world we understand is easier to look after.

4 Your wallet is your weapon: Check out the label and support things that look after the planet.

5 Ask others to help: Your school, adults you know, people like governments who can help change things.

6 Imagine different things: What would you want the world to be like when you are adults?

7 Give gifts and give thanks: Appreciate each other and be good to each other.

8 Get out more: In the garden, park, countryside - it's a great place.

9 Forgive yourself (and others): No one is perfect – just learn for next time.

10 Have fun: Looking after the world doesn't mean a dull life, it is a fabulous adventure.

11 Be the change you wish to see in the world: Lead by example. Not because a list has told you to but because it's how you want to be.

Word search

Find each word in the wordsearch - some are backwards, some are diagonal!

E	C	I	P	S	A	E	C	I	R
L	C	F	W	O	W	H	E	A	T
P	R	O	C	D	I	G	G	E	R
P	B	O	R	L	S	N	I	F	F
A	C	A	L	E	E	F	F	O	C
R	A	I	N	F	O	R	E	S	T
E	M	O	T	A	T	O	P	Z	A
G	R	A	P	E	N	O	M	E	L
E	N	E	D	E	N	A	E	B	A
B	E	E	R	M	A	I	Z	E	N
M	A	F	E	N	I	D	T	Z	B

ALAN
APPLE
BANANA
BEAN
BEER
CHILLI
COCOA
COFFEE
CORE
DIGGER
EDEN
ENID
GRAPE
LEMON
MAIZE
POTATO
RAINFOREST
RICE
SNIFF
SPICE
TEA
WHEAT

Answers

The Outdoor Biome

P4. COAL

P5. MICE

P6. YELLOW

P8. APPLE, HONEY,

VEGETABLES GROWN IN CORNWALL: Potatoes, cabbage, cauliflower (all year round) plus asparagus, courgettes, lettuce, beans, broccoli, tomatoes.

BARLEY and HOPS

P10. Plants are made into: Cars, canoes, fabrics, food, fuel, medicines, plastics, materials, packaging, pens, phone chargers, toys, houses, insulation, clothes, even fishing rods.

P11. Rocks give us: all the metals and stones we use every day. Anything that is not made of plants is probably mined. Buildings: concrete, bricks, blocks, metal roof of our Core. Inside buildings: pipes, electrical equipment, taps. Fuels and plastics from coal and oil. Machines: of all sizes. Glass, china clay for plates and making paper glossy, fertilizers.

P12. Medicine plants growing at Eden (in the winter they are sadly under the ground but their names are still in the little domes): Black Cohosh, Foxglove, Opium Poppy, Evening Primrose, Pot Marigold, Ginkgo, Feverfew, Elecampane, Echinacea, Globe Artichoke, Arnica, St. John's Wort.

Dyes: Red dye from madder. Blue dye from woad and indigo. Yellow dye from weld.

P14. WORM, WORD, CORD

The Core

P16. They make us fresh air to breathe: D

They keep our climate under control: E

They recycle our waste: A

They support animals and bugs (biodiversity): F

They clean our water: B

They give us ideas to copy (biomimicry): G

They suck CO_2 out of the air: C

They give us inspiration: H

P18. Across: 1: Digger, 5: Coco de Mer, 6: Banana.
Down: 2: Rubber, 3: Cocoa, 4: Weeeman

The Rainforest Biome

P21. Cocoa, Coffee, Bamboo, Mango, Banana

P22. SEA

P24. FIRE

P28/29. 1: B, 2: Keep Earth cool, control climate, give us food, fuel, medicine, materials, make rain and make oxygen (see SNIFF on p20), 4: A, B and C, 6: Putting on our wellies, 7: Banana, 8: Oil Palm, 9: Because rainforest are cut down to grow oil palm and the rainforests are the home of the orang-utang.

P30. A: Cloves, B: Ginger, C: Saffron, D: Vanilla, E: Pepper, F: Paprika

The Mediterranean Biome

P38. 1: Cork, 2: Stork, pig, 3: Peach, kiwi, loquat, apricot, feijoa, 4: Lemon, orange, lime, 5: Grape, 6: Dionysus, 7: Water, fertilizer, 8: Lighting lamps

P.T.O. for wordsearch answers.

Wordsearch answers

E	C	I	P	S	A	E	C	I	R
L	C	F	W	O	W	H	E	A	T
P	R	O	C	D	I	G	G	E	R
P	B	O	R	L	S	N	I	F	F
A	C	A	L	E	E	F	F	O	C
R	A	I	N	F	O	R	E	S	T
E	M	O	T	A	T	O	P	Z	A
G	R	A	P	E	N	O	M	E	L
E	N	E	D	E	N	A	E	B	A
B	E	E	R	M	A	I	Z	E	N
M	A	F	E	N	I	D	T	Z	B

THE CHILDREN'S GUIDE BOOK: THE EDEN TRAIL AN EDEN PROJECT BOOK 978 1 905 81195 3

Published in Great Britain by Eden Project Books, an imprint of Transworld Publishers A Random House Group Company

This edition published 2012

1 3 5 7 9 10 8 6 4 2

TRANSWORLD PUBLISHERS 61–63 Uxbridge Road, London W5 5SA

www.randomhousechildrens.co.uk www.edenproject.com

www.totallyrandombooks.co.uk www.randomhouse.co.uk

Addresses for companies within The Random House Group Limited can be found at: www.randomhouse.co.uk/offices.htm THE RANDOM HOUSE GROUP Limited Reg. No. 954009 A CIP catalogue record for this book is available from the British Library. The Eden Project is owned by the Eden Trust, A registered charity. Eden Project, Bodelva, St Austell, Cornwall, PL24 2SG

Printed and bound in Italy